A NIGHT WITHOUT DARKNESS

A Nephite Christmas Story

Written by Timothy Robinson
Illustrated by Jim Madsen

DESERET BOOK COMPANY
SALT LAKE CITY, UTAH

Momma and the other women told stories about Him. They spoke of One who would bring peace—the One who Samuel said would come when Samuel stood upon the wall and the arrows could not harm him.

Some of the women doubted and said they were just stories. But others said He would come and make the mighty and wicked men leave. HELAMAN 13:1–4; 14:2; 16:2

Some had dreams and said it would happen soon,
that there were miracles abroad in the land already.

And poor men whispered of angels and told glad tidings in darkened doorways. HELAMAN 16:13–14

But in the streets of Zarahemla, the children learned to hide when they heard hooves on the stone. They learned not to play too far from their own front doors and not to be out after dark. HELAMAN 16:22–23

Momma put me to bed early every night. She said it would not do for me to be up. "Dark things happen in dark times," she said. But from my window, before I went to sleep, I would count the stars in the northern sky and watch for the new star that Samuel had said would come. I wondered if I would notice it if it came. HELAMAN 14:3–7

Once, when I was playing ball with the other boys, I said how I had been counting stars. All the boys but one laughed at me and said that their fathers had told them such things were foolishness and to throw stones at anyone who counted stars and that they just might. HELAMAN 16:15–20

Then came the day when the notice appeared. It was written on a small, shiny piece of ziff, nailed by its corner to our door. The hammering woke me up, and I saw the scrap in my mother's trembling hand. She wouldn't read it to me. She wouldn't let me go outside. And it wasn't until later that morning, when the soldiers came in their armor for Father, that I realized what it said. 3 NEPHI 1:5–9

That night the soldiers brought Father home. He was dirty, and his robe was wet. When the soldiers left, Father said that he and the other men of the Church had been forced to gather wood all day. Dry wood from the forest. Kindling wood.

The men had been ordered to make a huge pile of wood in the center of town. Father said that we weren't to leave our house. He said that if the signs Samuel had spoken of—the new star and the night without darkness— didn't come by morning after next, something terrible would happen. 3 NEPHI 1:9–11

We knelt in a circle and prayed, each of us in turn, until my knees hurt so much I couldn't kneel anymore and had to sit on the floor. Still we prayed. And it was dark.

The next day seemed to last forever—a day without school, without work, without play. Father told us that the prophet Nephi had prophesied we would be safe. Father said that we needed to have faith in Nephi's promise. But I was still scared, and I knew that Momma was too.

We sat in our house, hearing the clatter of the horses' hooves on the stones of the street, listening to the low voices of the soldiers who passed outside our door. Momma held me and stroked my hair. She got up to get some food for me, but I wasn't hungry.

That evening we prayed again. Then we gathered at the window in our kitchen, the one that faces west. We sat in silence and watched as the sun crept down against the mountains . . . sinking, sinking, sinking. And the mountains looked orange against it. 3 NEPHI 1:12–13

I felt my heart burn within me. Momma held me, her arm warm against my chest. And as the tip of the sun's fire took its last peek over the hills, I knew. The sun disappeared, but the air was still bright. "Momma!" I cried. "Momma, it came!" I got up and ran to my bedroom. There, framed in the window by my bed, was the star, so bright I could have seen it at midday. 3 NEPHI 1:15, 20–21

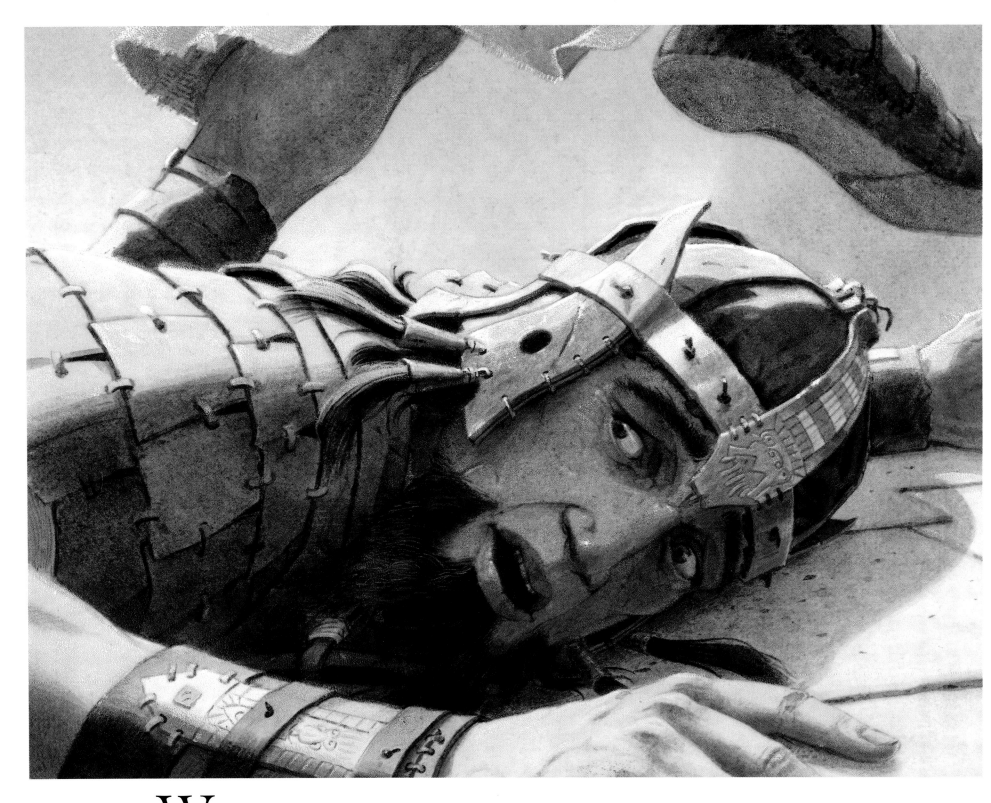

We poured into the street. We didn't fear the soldiers by our door. They had fallen to the ground with their hands to their eyes. Father stepped over them and began running, and Momma and I ran after him, all the way to the center of town.

And there, in the square by the big pile of wood, were other men and women, girls and boys, holding hands and singing—singing hymns to the Lord, to Him who would be crucified and not be spared. 3 NEPHI 1:16; ROMANS 8:32

Later, the prophet Nephi led us down to the river. He baptized all who would believe, and there were crowds of people standing on the riverbank, under the trees. Hundreds of people waiting and soldiers taking off their breastplates. 3 NEPHI 1:23

Before long, it seemed, the sun rose again, and the crowd grew quiet to see it. They stood on the land and in the water and watched it rising in the east, as if it were the coming of morning. 3 NEPHI 1:19

I crept onto my mother's lap and quietly fell asleep. And as I slept, I dreamt of a little baby boy crying on a hillside, surrounded by sheep. The skies above Him were filled with new stars, and each seemed to be an angel, each holding its arms out and singing, "Behold, He cometh unto His own." 3 NEPHI 1:14; LUKE 2:7–12

For Ethan and Nate
May you always love Book of Mormon stories

—TR

For Mckenzie, Hannah, and Easton
and for my wife, Holly

—JM

Library of Congress Cataloging-in-Publication Data

Robinson, Timothy M., 1967–
    A night without darkness / Timothy M. Robinson ; illustrations by
James Allen Madsen.
        p.   cm.
    Summary: Recounts the miracle, from the Book of Mormon, of a night
without darkness, which made known the birth of Christ to the
inhabitants of North and South America.
    ISBN 1-57345-504-0
    1. Jesus Christ—Nativity Juvenile literature.   2. Church of Jesus
Christ of Latter-day Saints—Doctrines Juvenile literature.
[1. Jesus Christ—Nativity.   2. Book of Mormon stories.]
I. Madsen, James Allen, 1964–   ill.   II. Title.
BX8643.J4R63   1999
289.3'22—dc21   99-33984
                                                            CIP

Printed in Mexico   18961-6509

10   9   8   7   6   5   4   3   2   1